The Hidden Way

Celtic Prayers for the Spiritual Journey

The Hidden Way

Celtic Prayers for the Spiritual Journey

RAY SIMPSON

Copyright © 2023, Anamchara Books.

All rights reserved. No part of this publication may be reproduced or transmitted for commercial purposes, except for brief quotations, without written permission of the publisher. Churches and other noncommercial interests may reproduce portions of this book without the express written permission of Anamchara Books, provided that the text does not exceed 500 words or 5 percent of the entire book, whichever is less, and that the text is not material quoted from another publisher. When reproducing text from this book, include the following credit line: "From *The Hidden Way: Celtic Prayers for the Spiritual Journey*, published by Anamchara Books. Used by permission."

Vestal, New York 13850

www.AnamcharaBooks.com

paperback ISBN: 978-1-62524-851-0

eBook ISBN: 978-1-62524-872-5

All scripture quotations are Anamchara Books' literal interpretation based on Hebrew and Greek lexicons.

Quotations from the saints and other historical authors have, in some cases, been slightly altered to allow for inclusive language.

Cover by Ellyn Sanna.

Interior design by Micaela Grace.

Knowing One of the hidden path,

Infinite One of the wise heart,

Saving One of the clear sight,

may I learn from you as an eager pupil;

may I learn from life as a humble child;

may I learn from night, may I learn from day;

may I learn from soul friends,

may I learn from stillness.

Show me your hidden path.

CONTENTS

INTRODUCTION ... 9

I. THE SPIRIT AND ITS FRUITS 13

1. SPIRIT ... 15
2. STRENGTH TO LOVE ... 27
3. PEACE ... 49
4. WISDOM ... 69
5. FREEDOM ... 87

II. LOVE'S SETTINGS ... 95

6. RELATIONSHIPS ... 97
7. COMMUNITY ... 109
8. THE WORLD OF NATURE ... 121

III. LOVE'S RESULTS ... 129

9. RENEWAL ... 131
10. WALKING IN THE PROMISE ... 145
11. ETERNITY ... 153

INTRODUCTION

"**Even if all the doors are closed,**" wrote Rumi, "a secret path will be there for you that no one knows. You can't see it yet but so many paradises are at the end of this path."

Ray Simpson understands the meaning of Rumi's words. He knows the thirteenth-century poet wasn't talking about the selfish satisfaction that comes from fame, power, financial wealth, or the accumulation of material things. Instead, like Rumi, Ray has spent his life following the mystic's path that lies hidden in the midst of everyday life, leading deeper and deeper into the living Presence of God.

Ray speaks as one who has followed the Celtic path for most of his life. Although there are many definitions of the word *Celtic*, for Ray, the heart of Celtic Christianity is simply following the Way of Christ in the everyday, ordinariness of life—getting up in the morning and going to bed at night, going to work and playing with children, suffering pain and rejoicing in pleasure, working together in friendships and families and communities.

This ancient way is not unique to the Celts, of course, for it has been known and followed by all God-seekers down through the centuries (as the quotations at the beginning of each section of this book demonstrate). When we follow this path, the living Spirit is our companion, filling our lives with spiritual "fruit," the natural consequences of our relationship with God. This is the way of love, which brings us strength, peace, wisdom, and freedom—and empowers us to spread these qualities to the world around us.

When we speak of love in connection to the mystic's hidden way, we are not adding something new to it, for the hidden path is itself the way of love—love of God, love of other human beings, and love of all Creation, including our own selves. As the Desert Father Isaac of Nineveh wrote in the seventh century,

> Love is the kingdom of which our Lord spoke when He symbolically promised the disciples that they would eat in His kingdom: "you shall eat and drink at the table of my kingdom." What should they eat, if not love? Love is ... the wine that gladdens the human heart. Blessed is everyone who has drunk from this wine. This is the wine from which the selfish have drunk, and they became pure; ... the poor, and they became rich in hope; the sick, and they became valiant; the fools, and they became wise.

Three centuries earlier, John Chrysostom, one of the Early Church Fathers, also knew love is central to the Divine Way.

> Love is the mother of all blessings, their root and source; it is the end of wars and the extermination of strife. Indeed, just as dissent and strife cause death and demise prematurely, so love and harmony produce peace and unanimity, and where there is peace and unanimity, all in life is safe and secure. Why speak

of the present only? Love brings us heaven and inexpressible benefits; it is the queen of virtues.

Love, the Way of God that weaves through all Reality, is embodied in intimate relationships, in communities, and in the world of Nature. It brings renewal to souls and cells and societies. It allows us to walk confidently, even when the way ahead is obscured, for this is the Path of Promise, which leads through the ordinary details of each day, so that this life participates in eternity.

Come, then. Join Ray Simpson in prayer as you follow the *hidden way* to Life.

—*Anamchara Books*

I

THE SPIRIT AND ITS FRUITS

The fruit of the Spirit are love, delight, wholeness,
patience, active kindness, useful goodness,
gentle strength, and self-control.

—Galatians 5:22–23

1
SPIRIT

The Spirit of glory and God
rests on you and refreshes you.

—1 Peter 4:14

Holy Spirit, the life that gives life:
You are the cause of all movement.
You are the breath of all creatures.
You are the salve that gives health to our souls.
You are the ointment that heals our wounds.
You are the fire that warms our hearts.
You are the light that guides our feet.
Let all the world praise you.

—Hildegard of Bingen (twelfth century)

Open the window of your heart
and let the Spirit speak.

—Rumi (thirteenth century)

The Breath of the Spirit

O King of the Tree of Life,
the blossoms on the branches are your people.
The singing birds are your angels;
the whispering breeze is your Spirit.
O King of the Tree of Life,
may the blossoms bring forth the sweetest fruit.
May the birds sing out the highest praise;
may your Spirit cover all with her gentle breath.

Spirit Light

Come, Holy Spirit,
from heaven shine forth
with your glorious light!
Most kindly, warming Light,
enter the inmost depths of our hearts.
Thaw that which is frozen, kindle our energy,
burn away our apathy, illumine our path.

Energy for the Struggle

Spirit whose breath
gives energy for struggle,
set us free to grow as the children of God.
Open our ears
that we may hear the weeping of the world.
Open our mouths
that we may be a voice for the voiceless.
Open our eyes that we may discern
your just and gentle ways.
Open our hearts
that we may bring courage and love to life.

Come, Spirit!

Come like the fire
and kindle love in our hearts.
Come like the winds
and breathe fresh life into our frames.
Come like the tides
and immerse us in your presence.
Come from the Earth
to sustain and nourish our being.

Spirit Flow

O God, we see your story
in flowing streams,
in people's dreams, in sporting teams.
As the water in the stream
makes its journey to the sea,
so we will flow with your Spirit
and with your saints,
on to you.

(echoes a New Zealand prayer)

Bedtime Prayer

May the Spirit pour upon us as we sleep,
work in us as we dream,
take the frowns from our brows,
and wake us up refreshed.
The blessing of the perfect Spirit be ours.
The blessing of the Three be pouring on us,
graciously and generously,
hour by hour.

Filled with the Spirit

Spirit of God,
the breath of Creation is yours.
Spirit of God,
the groans of the world are yours.
Spirit of God,
the wonder of communion is yours.
Spirit of God,
the fire of love is yours,
and we are filled.

The River of the Spirit

Come to us with your anointing power.
Anoint us as you will for the ministries you will.
God of the call, God of the journey,
thank you for your anointing
of Barnabas, Columba,
and so many other of your saints,
from the Day of Pentecost until now.
Holy Spirit, our strong cord,
may your fiber weave through our lives.
Rain of God, revive our withered hearts.
Wind of God, blow us where you will.
Breeze of God, refresh us with your love.
River of God, flow through us and heal our land.
River of God, flow through us and heal our land.

Prayer Before Eating

Holy Spirit of God,
you are the source of all that lives,
of all that grows,
of all that provides us with food.
May we know your presence with us
as we share this meal.

Wild Spirit

Spirit of God, be wild and free in me.
Batter my proud and stubborn will.
Blow me where you choose.
Break me down if you must.
Re-fashion me as you will.
Move me powerfully away
from the games I play
in order to try to tame you.
Lead me into the wild places,
the places of dream or scream,
the new frontiers or the total quiet,
the long dark tunnels or the wide, sunny vistas,
to speak to lions, to move
mountains, to bear tragedy,
to mirror you.

Holy Wind

Wind, wind, blow on me.
Blow away the cobwebs that clog my spirit.
Blow up the suffocating clouds of unbelief.
Blow me near things that are pure and good.
Blow me along the path of your choice.
Blow through me the breath of God's presence.

2
STRENGTH TO LOVE

Happy is the person whose strength comes from God.
Their inner being will be like a highway, leading to life. . . .
They walk from strength into greater strength.

—Psalm 84:5, 7

There is love like a small lamp,
which goes out when the oil is consumed;
or like a stream which dries up when it doesn't rain.
But there is a love that is like a mighty spring
gushing up out of the earth;
it keeps flowing forever, and is inexhaustible.

—Isaac of Nineveh (seventh century)

The proof of love is in the works.
Where love exists, it works great things.
But when it ceases to act, it ceases to exist.

—Gregory the Great (sixth century)

Lift Us Up

Lift us up
in our tiredness.
Lift us up
in disappointment.
Lift us up.
Lift us, Lord,
out of darkness into light,
out of despair into hope.
Lift us, Lord,
out of sadness into joy,
out of failure into trust.
Lift us, Lord,
out of anger into forgiveness,
out of pride into freedom.

The Strength of Defenseless Love

Babe of heaven, defenseless Love,
you had to travel far from your home.
Strengthen us on our pilgrimage of trust.
King of glory, you accepted such humbling;
clothe us with the garments of humility.
Your birth shows us the simplicity
of the Creator's love;
keep us in the simplicity of that love.
Your coming shows us the
wonder of being human;
help us to cherish every human life.

(echoes a prayer of George Appleton)

Strong Hope

Bless to us this day of joy.
Open to us heaven's generous gates.
Strengthen our hope.
Revive our tired souls,
till we sing the joys of your glory
with all the angels of heaven.
Hold also
those who are sleeping rough,
those who feel shut out of society,
those who are cold and hungry,
and these we name before you now.

On the Shepherd's Shoulders

You who lift the lowly
and strengthen the frail,
who in your weakness raised a fallen world
and let sinners lift you onto a cross,
we thank you.
Lift each of us on to your shoulders,
like a shepherd
who does not neglect one lost sheep.
Lift us from earth to heaven.

This Day

On this day, Spirit of Energy,
establish your vibrancy in our beings.
On this day, Spirit of Power,
establish your strength in our frames.
On this day, Spirit of Love,
establish your goodness in our hearts.

Claiming God's Strength

You who put life in wheat and lamb,
you who put heaven in bread and wine,
send us out in your strength
to bring heaven on earth.

We Arise

We arise today
in the strength of the mighty Creator,
in the strength of the rising Saviour,
in the strength of the life-giving Spirit,
in the strength of the mighty Three
whose love is One.
We arise today
in the strength of the angels and archangels,
in the strength of the prophets and apostles,
in the strength of the martyrs and saints.
We arise today
in the strength of heaven and earth,
in the strength of sun and moon,
in the strength of fire and wind.
We arise today
in the strength of Christ's birth and baptism,
in the strength of Christ's death and rising,
in the strength of Christ's judgement to come.

Fortified from Within

Strength-giver,

may your fiber weave us together.

Fortifier,

may your praises swell in us.

Indweller,

may your presence dwell in us.

Clothed in Strength

We rise up clothed in the strength of Christ.
We shall not be imprisoned,
we shall not be harmed.
We shall not be downtrodden,
we shall not be left alone.
We shall not be tainted,
we shall not be overwhelmed.
We go clothed in Christ's white garments.
We go freed to weave Christ's patterns.
We go loved to serve Christ's weak ones.

Strong for Justice

God of community,
Spirit of energy and change,
pour on us without reserve or distinction,
that we may have strength
to plant your justice on earth.

Strength
with Wisdom and Compassion

Lord, we offer you this day's troubles.

Give us

strength to bear them,

wisdom to handle them,

compassion for those who brought them,

peace as to their outcome.

Quietness and Confidence

Aware One,

quiet our fevered minds.

subdue our overheated souls,

and rest our stressed bodies.

In quietness and confidence be our strength.

Strength in Weakness

Jesus, when we are weak,
remind us that your strength
can reach others through our weakness.
Open our eyes to notice what you notice.
Open our mouths
to speak one healing, life-giving word.

Strength to Leave Behind

Guide us, our great Mentor,
through the ups and downs of life.
Strengthen us to leave behind
all that hinders our calling,
and to keep moving
toward ever-greater reality.

Our Greatest Weakness

Christ of enduring love,
take us to our point of greatest weakness,
and let us find you there.
May your strength
be made complete in our frailty.

Strong Roots

Holy God, loving and mighty,
strip from me
all that is false and out of place;
strengthen my roots in you;
bring me to that place
where I desire you alone.

The Sweet, Strong Center

Irresistible One,
when the world falls apart,
be our Center.
When the world turns sour,
be our Sweetness.
When we become weak,
be our Strength.

Walking in Strength

We walk in the strength
of the mighty Three in One:
the Creator who cares for us,
the Saviour beside us,
the Spirit who makes us strong.

Strength for the Unknown

Lord, be within us to give us strength,
over us to protect us,
beneath us to support us,
in front of us to be our guide,
behind us to catch us if we fall,
surrounding us to give us courage;
so that alone, alone,
we may walk into
the great unknown.

Prayer Before a Meal

May this food restore our strength,

give new energy to tired limbs,

new thoughts to weary minds.

May this drink restore our souls,

give new vision to dry spirits,

new warmth to cold hearts.

And, once refreshed,

may we give new pleasure to you,

who gives all to us.

3
PEACE

I give you my peace.

—Jesus (John 14:27)

*We have come in accordance with the counsels of Jesus
to cut down our warlike and arrogant swords of argument
into ploughshares, and we convert into sickles
the spears we formerly used in fighting...
having become children of peace for the sake of Jesus,*

—Origen (third century)

*When peace dwells in our hearts it enables us
to contemplate the grace of the Holy Spirit from within.
When we dwell in peace,
we collect spiritual gifts as it were with a scoop,
and we shed the light of knowledge on others....
When we live in peace, God reveals mysteries to us.*

—Seraphim of Sarov (eighteenth century)

Inner and Outer Peace

Deep peace of the Creator
be between you and all creatures.
Deep peace of the Saviour
be between you and all people.
Deep peace of the Spirit
be between you
and all that is within you.

Circled with Peace

All-powerful God, circle the places
where dark or distracting forces now gather.
Circle the groups in thrall to
phantoms and ghouls.
May fears diminish and peace increase,
for yours is the kingdom,
the power and the glory,
for ever and ever.
Amen.

Peace Above all Peace

Peace between victor and vanquished.
Peace between us and all people.
Peace of Christ above all peace.

The Fabric of This Day

We weave this day:

silence of knowing,

clearness of seeing, grace of speaking.

We weave this day:

humility of listening,

depth of understanding, joy of serving.

We weave this day:

peace of being,

gift of loving, power of meeting.

May peace be woven through

the fabric of this day.

Deep Peace

Lead us from death to life,
from falsehood to truth.
Lead us from despair to hope,
from fear to trust.
Lead us from hate to love,
from war to peace.
Deep peace of the Son of peace,
fill our hearts, our workplaces, our world.

(echoes the Universal Prayer for Peace)

The Peace of God's Presence

Good God,

be with us in every experience of life.

When we neglect you,

remind us of your presence;

when we are frightened,

give us courage;

when we are tempted,

give us the power to resist;

when we are anxious and worried,

give us peace;

when we are weary in service,

renew our tired frame.

The Light of Peace

Perfect Comforter!
Wonderful Refreshment!
You make peace dwell in our souls.
In our labours, you offer rest;
in temptation, strength.
From heaven shine forth
the glorious light
of your peace.

The Peace of the Father's Will

Lord Jesus,
in the midst of mockery and madness,
you found peace
and remained in your Father's will.
In the middle of fretful day,
give us also peace
to remain in our Father's will.

The Divine Peace Embedded in Life

O Being of life!
O Being of peace!
O Being of time!
You are present with us.

Peace of All Peace

May the Light of lights
come to our dark hearts;
may the Spirit's wisdom
come to us from our Saviour.
May the peace of the Spirit be ours,
the peace of the Son,
the peace of the Creator,
the peace of all peace be ours.

The Source of Peace

The Creator

who brought order out of chaos,

give peace to us.

The Saviour

who calmed the raging sea,

give peace to us.

The Spirit

who broods upon the deeps,

give peace to us.

Heaven's Peacekeepers

May heaven's peacekeepers
encircle us all with their outstretched arms;
to protect us from the hostile powers;
to put balm into our dreams;
to give us contented, sweet repose.

Prayer Before Sleeping

We lie down in peace,

knowing our sins are forgiven.

We lie down in peace,

knowing death has no fear.

We lie down in peace,

knowing no powers can harm us.

We lie down in peace, knowing Jesus is near.

Peace be upon our breath.

Peace be upon our eyes.

Peace be upon our sleep.

Nighttime Prayer

The peace of the Spirit be ours this night,
the peace of Jesus be ours this night,
the peace of the Creator be ours this night,
the peace that rules Heaven be ours this night,
each morning and evening of our lives.

Peace for the Workplace

Worker Christ, as we enter our workplace,
may we bring your presence with us.
Grace us to speak your peace
and bring order into our work atmosphere.
Remind us to acknowledge your authority
over all that will be thought, decided,
and accomplished within this place.
Give us a fresh supply of truth and beauty
on which to draw as we work.

(echoes a prayer of Julia McGuinness)

Living at Peace

Loving One,
help me to understand my own story,
to fear nothing except fear itself,
and to live at peace
with myself, the creatures you have made,
and the entire world.

Healing Peace

Rain grace on us and heal us,
and we shall lie down in peace.
Rain grace on us and heal us,
and we shall lie down in peace

The Fruit of Constant Endeavour

Source of Peace,

war is the price we pay

for the selfishness of nations:

Help us to wage endless war against selfishness.

Peace is the fruit of constant

endeavour for the good:

Help us to struggle without ceasing

for good to triumph over evil.

4
WISDOM

*Heaven's primordial wisdom has holiness as its priority,
then peacefulness, justice, tolerance, reason.
It is full of compassion and positive consequences,
wholehearted, free from hidden agendas.*

—James 3:18

*Intellect is the knowledge
obtained by experience of names and forms;
wisdom is the knowledge
which manifests only from the inner being....
Intellect is the sight which enables one to see
through the external world,
but the light of wisdom enables one to see
through the external into the internal world.*

—Hazrat Inayat Khan (nineteenth century)

Encompassing Wisdom

Come to us, Wisdom,
moving in the flux and flow of the cosmos
to bring worlds into being.
Come to us, Wisdom,
permeating all Creation,
the life of soil and seed and seasons.
Come to us, Wisdom,
shaping nations and ensouling peoples.
Come to us, Wisdom,
encompassing the mysteries of the unseen world
and the mysteries of the soul.
Come to us, Wisdom,
the seeing eye of art and science,
the ear of all that breathes.
Come to us, Wisdom,
the light of our darkness,
the reconciler of that which is divided.
Come to us, Wisdom,
the weaver of Earth's destiny,
the completer of our call.

The Mind of God

Wisdom,

permeating Creation,

informing all peoples,

come and bring us the mind of God.

True Fulfiller-of-Desire,

harness our deepest longings

to your infinite purpose of love.

God-with-Us,

the Presence that cannot be taken from us,

may we live with you

and may you live in us

forever.

Wise Saint Hilda

God our Wisdom,
who set Hilda as a mother in the Church,
may we now delight to claim her gifts of wisdom:
the wisdom of silence
and the wisdom of speech;
the wisdom of observation
and the wisdom of revealing;
the wisdom of memory
and the wisdom of work;
the wisdom of deeds
and the wisdom of being.

(Hilda of Whitby, who lived in the seventh century, brought the teachings of Christ to Anglo-Saxon England. She was the abbess of several convents and recognized for the wisdom that drew kings to her for advice.)

Like an Oak Tree

May I be like an oak tree of wisdom
with my roots deep in the soil of holy reflection.
May my reach be high,
wide and hospitable to all.
May I be strong to withstand gales,
may my life be rich with nuts of wisdom,
and may I birth many oaklings,
seeds of your wisdom, O Spirit of All Wisdom.

Wisdom in the Silence

Word of God,
out of the silence of eternity
you ceaselessly speak to your children.
Teach us to listen,
not to the discordant babble of a sick society,
but to the treasures of truth,
the holy wisdom that rings forth
in the deeps of silence.

Wisdom to Act

Carpenter Christ, give us common sense
and save us from a life of nonsense.
Help us to discern where circumstances
herald rather than hinder
your unfolding purpose.
Speak through Nature,
prick our consciences,
and make us aware of what we
are on this earth for.
Then, Jesus, prompt us to take the next step.

Wise Discernment

God of wisdom, give us good judgement.
Help us to distinguish:
that which confuses
from that which brings light;
that which brings peace
from that which brings strife;
that which brings reality
from that which is illusion;
that which builds love
from that which feeds distrust.

Divine Truth

Life-Giver, grant me the strength
to do without things.
Grant me the wisdom
to see the "within" of things.
Grant me the knowledge
to take the measure of evil spirits.
Grant me understanding
to know your Truth.

The Wisdom of the Scriptures

All-seeing God,

who has given to us the Holy Scriptures,

help us so to value them,

to read, mark, learn, and inwardly digest them,

that we may grow in wisdom

and in understanding of your ways,

now and for eternity.

Prayer Before Reading the Bible

Risen Christ, as we read this passage,

may we be aware that you are here with us.

Eternal truth flows through the words we read.

You know the particular word

that we most need now.

We open ourselves to you.

Please speak to us.

Reveal your wisdom.

Wise Practices

God of Wisdom, teach us
to use our minds well,
study with a humble heart,
relate the parts to the whole,
explore things with wonder,
listen to those who know more than we do,
and learn from our mistakes.

Learning

All-Knowing God,
make fruitful our learning.
May we acquire information
that forms us for a good purpose
and does not distract us from it.
May we link up what we learn today
with what we already know,
and so become more whole.
May we offer to you in love what we learn,
so that it shows in our words,
our silences, and our actions.

Growing Wisdom

Divine Source of Truth,
Beauty, and Goodness,
our minds are like a field.
In this field, please grow many good things,
many beautiful things,
and many true things with deep roots.
Teach us also how to weed and sift and sort,
how to water and prune wisely.

Timely Wisdom

Living One,
help us to think things through,
to sense the season,
and to relate what we do
to the signs of the times.
Help us to act and speak appropriately.

Prayer at the End of the Day

Examine me, O God,
and know my inner feelings.
Reveal to me the cause
of any divided or angry thoughts.
I place today's failures and frustrations
into your hands.
I give thanks to you for all my blessings.
Take what I have learned today,
and work in me even as I sleep,
that tomorrow I may be
more effective as a human being.

Reshaped, Cleansed, and Healed

Bend our minds to holy learning.
Give us wisdom to know the nub of things,
memory to recall the important things,
and clarity to express what we learn.
May your truth reshape us
and may we always walk humbly in the light.
We pray for the cleansing of our perceptions,
that we may hear, that we may see,
that we may understand with our hearts,
and that we may be healed.

Humility and Wisdom

Teach us, dear God, to
know your ways,
explore your world,
learn from mistakes,
understand people,
manage time and talents,
weave meaning out of memory,
gain insight from inspired people,
and grow into the stature of Christ.
Unlock for us, Life-Giver,
the treasures of wisdom,
but first give us hearts for humble learning.

5
FREEDOM

*You were called to freedom,
but do not use your freedom
as a starting place for selfishness
but rather, because of love, serve others.*

—Galatians 5:13

*Let this reality settle into your bones,
and allow your soul the freedom
to sing, dance, praise and love.*

—Teresa of Avila (seventeenth century)

*Freedom and happiness of soul
consist in detachment from transitory things.*

—Anthony Abbot (third century)

Freed from False Desire

Lead us into the desert of purging
that through reflection and prayer
we may leave behind
the things that tie our spirits down
and learn again to be your pilgrim people.
Through fasting from the frenzied feeding
of false desires,
through study of your word,
meditation, and acts of service,
restore the clearness of our seeing
and free us to share your generous love with all.

The Freedom of Christ

Saving Christ,

by your incarnation and birth in poverty,

set us free.

By your prayers and self-discipline,

set us free.

By your tender works of mercy,

set us free.

By your struggle for truth and justice,

set us free.

By your nobility in persecution,

set us free.

By your self-giving even in death,

set us free.

Free to Dance

Thrice holy God,
bring us to life.
Call us to freedom.
Move between us with your love.
Free us from all that holds us back,
so that today may we participate
in the dance of your Trinity,
so that our lives resonate with yours.

Freed to Flower

May the presence
of the Three Kindly Persons
free each of us to accept personal pain,
to grow through each stage of development,
to give space to others,
to express feelings,
to forgive from the heart,
to flower as a person.

Courageous Freedom

O Spirit, be free in us.
Let us not bind you through fear
of where your disturbing power will lead.
Burst through these brittle shells;
shake us to the foundations;
strip us to the core,
which is our essence and your love.
Give us the courage to share your freedom.

Freed From the Past

Lord Jesus,
in your name I break the power of the past.
May it no longer have a hold over me.
May the cross of Christ
come between me and my past.
May the love of Jesus fill me,
for I am a lamb of your choosing,
so that I may rest in your arms
and walk free into the fruitful paths
you have in store for me.

Protected

Be with us now, Living One.
Keep us in your presence, power, and peace,
and may the saints and the angels watch over us.
Compassionate God of heaven's powers,
screen us from people with evil intentions.
Compassionate God of freedom,
free us from curses and spells.
Compassionate God of eternity,
free this place from bad influences of the past.
Protect us from all that would chain us
or hold us captive,
so that we may be free to sing and serve.

II
LOVE'S SETTINGS

God is perfect, faultless.
And so, when Divine love becomes manifest in us
in the fullness of Grace, we radiate this love—
not only on the earth, but throughout
the entire universe as well.
So God is in us and is present everywhere.
It is God's all-encompassing love
that manifests itself in us.
When this happens, we see no difference between people:
everyone is good, everyone is kin,
and we consider ourselves to be servants
of every created thing.

—Elder Thaddeus (twentieth century)

6

RELATIONSHIPS

Love doesn't give up easily;
it is kind and gentle; it doesn't envy or lust;
it doesn't boast or brag; it isn't puffed up with itself;
... it doesn't try to get its own way;
it doesn't take things personally;
it doesn't dwell on past wrongs....
Love puts up with annoyances, believes the best,
never stops hoping, and always endures.

—1 Corinthians 13:4–5, 7

Let us draw close to each other.
Let us be other-loving rather than self-loving.

—Gregory the Theologian (fourth century)

Your task is not to seek for love, but merely to seek and find
all the barriers within yourself that you have built against it.

—Rumi (thirteenth century)

Prayer for a Relationship

May failures be forgiven,

wounds be healed,

confusions be resolved,

ignorance be dispelled,

this relationship be treasured.

The Trinity

When relationship is difficult,
remind us, great Three-in-One,
that we arise today in a mighty force:
the God who is One,
the God who is Three,
creating all through love.
We arise today
in the strength of the Creator,
in the gentleness of Jesus,
in the flow of the Spirit,
affirming all through love.

Little Trinities

Thank you for the little trinities
that reflect to us your nature:
for love-making, conceiving, and nurturing;
for body, mind, and soul;
for the fellowship of races, airwaves, and sport.

Reshaped Relationships

We grieve that we who are made
to reflect your three-fold love
have violated our nature and yours.
We have not reflected
the Father's heart of the Creator.
We have not reflected
the Mother's heart of the Saviour.
We have not reflected
the Soul-friend's heart of the Spirit.
Holy and immortal One, have mercy upon us.
Reshape our relationships into your image.

Reflections of the Trinity

Eternal Love Maker,
Eternal Love Mate,
Eternal Love Messenger,
Three of limitless love,
we glimpse your reflection in
a tender kiss, a warm embrace,
sporting comradeship,
an adult affirming a child, a meal shared,
two people listening to each other,
a group making music, hospitality,
young people serving the old,
Black and white people forming friendships.
Three of limitless love,
may we reflect more of you
in whose likeness we are made.

Relationship with God

God who walks with your people
and communed with Enoch,
teach us also to walk in intimacy with you,
fleeing from everything
that clouds our relationship,
until even death is but a gentle passing over
into your nearer presence.

Our Role Model

Jesus, you are our role model,
showing us what real friendship looks like.
You call us to love the way you loved,
setting aside our selfish preoccupations
so that we may serve one another.

The Presence of Jesus

Where two or three are gathered together,
you promised to be present.
Be present, Jesus, in each of our relationships:
lovers, friends, families.
May we sense your Spirit,
and may others see your love
through us.

The Nature of God

Three-in-One,
we know that friendship is your very nature.
You are one Love,
expressed as three eternally loving Selves,
who constantly lay down their lives for each other,
just as Jesus did for us.

The Paraclete

Holy Spirit, you are the Paraclete,
who walks beside me,
who is linked to me,
who stands with me,
whose love is unconditional.
May I demonstrate this same faithfulness
in my loyalty to my friends.

7
COMMUNITY

Together you are the body of Christ.
Each of you have your own role to play in that body.

—1 Corinthians 12:27

We who formerly treasured money and possessions
more than anything else now hand over everything we have
to a treasury for all and share it with everyone who needs it.
We who formerly hated and murdered one another
now live together and share the same table.
We pray for our enemies and try to win those who hate us.

—Justin the Martyr (second century)

We are already one.
But we imagine that we are not.
And what we have to recover is our original unity.
What we have to be is what we are.

—Thomas Merton (twentieth century)

Diversity and Unity

God who is One,

you create us in diversity.

God who is Three,

draw us into unity.

The Jesus of Community

Jesus, broken on the cross,
we bring to you those suffering from broken dreams,
broken relationships, and broken promises.
Jesus, have mercy on them.
Jesus, who lost everything, we bring to you
those who have suffered loss of work,
mobility, and well-being.
Jesus, have mercy on them.
Jesus, defenseless victim, we bring to you
those who are victims of violence, abuse,
and false accusation.
Jesus, have mercy on them.
Jesus, alone and destitute, we bring to you
those who are lonely, homeless, and hungry.
Jesus, have mercy on them.
Jesus, you died that we may be brought back to you.
Save and raise up
those who have none but you to turn to.
Jesus, have mercy on them.

The Eternal Realm of Love

Teach us to leave behind
prejudice and meanness of spirit.
Incite us to generous giving.
Help us to create space for you
and play our part
in the eternal realm of your love.

Spirit Life

Spirit of God,
the breath of Creation is yours.
Spirit of God,
the groans of the world are yours.
Spirit of God,
the wonder of communion is yours.
Spirit of God,
you live within our communities,
and we are filled.

Unity in Diversity

Birther who brought worlds into being,
bring your purpose to birth in us.
Saviour who reconnected
an estranged world to its Source,
reconnect us to our Source.
Spirit who breathes through everything that lives,
breathe fully through us.
Triune God who delights to
bring diversity in unity,
bring unity to our diversity.

New Birth

May the life of the Three
give birth to new creativity.
May the yielding of the Three
give birth to a new society.
May the love of the Three
give birth to new community.

Light-Bringer

Shaper of peoples,
who through Moses gave guidance
that would make a people great,
guide us into the ways of true greatness.
Bedrock, Sign of Community,
come to places of instability
and root them in realities
that nothing can destroy.
Key to Destiny, unlock our potential
and our capacity to befriend and serve others,
that we may be mentors and soul friends
amid a needy people.
Light-Bringer, illumine places of darkness,
despair, and disease.
May we too carry your light
so that it spreads out through our community.

Weeping with God

Open our eyes, that we may weep with you.
May we weep with you for the blindness of pride
that corrodes the dignity of human life.
Open our eyes, that we may weep with you.
We weep with you over the mad rush to consume
that tramples down the Earth and her children.
Open our eyes, that we may weep with you.
We weep with you for the lust to control that
imprisons the soul and fragments community.
Open our eyes, that we may weep with you.

The Presence of the Life-Giver

Life-Giver, we offer you all we are,
all we have, all we do,
and all whom we shall meet this day,
that you will be given the glory.
We offer you our homes and work,
our schools and leisure,
and everyone in our community today;
may all be done as if for you.
We offer you the broken and hungry;
may the wealth and work of the world
be available to all and for the exploitation of none.
May your presence be known to all.

In God's Hands

Into your hands, O Loving One,
we place our families, our neighbours,
our brothers and sisters in Christ,
and all whom we have met today:
enfold them in your will.
Into your hands, O Just One,
we place all who are victims of prejudice,
oppression, or neglect;
the unwanted, the frail.
May everyone be cherished
from conception to the grave.
Into your hands, O Healing One,
we place all who are restless,
sick, or prey to the powers of evil.
Into your hands, O Guarding One,
we place these members of our community.
Watch over them.

Defenseless Love

God of Community,
bring to birth a community of justice.
We pray for the powerful,
who impose their will on the weak;
may they come to know your defenseless love.
We pray for those who seek revenge
through acts of terror;
may they come to know your defenseless love.
We pray for those who have
lost limbs or loved ones;
may they come to know your defenseless love.

8
THE WORLD OF NATURE

*The stars and galaxies
tell the story of Divine abundance and light.
Their expanse reveals Divine handicraft.
Meaning bubbles up from each day,
and night after night imprints God's message on our senses.*

—Psalm 19:1–2.

*Let the sky be happy!
Let the Earth cry out with joy!
Let the sea thunder, with all its vast abundance;
let the fields and all that live within them be jubilant;
may all the trees in the forest raise their voices
in a ringing cry of joy!*

—Psalm 96:11–12

The whole Earth is a living icon of the face of God.

—John of Damascus (seventh century)

The Presence of God

We bless you, God, for the sun:
its source of fire, its beams of light,
its rays of warmth.
We bless you, God, for water:
when it is ice, when it is steam,
when it is flowing free.
We bless you, God, for a human being:
the thinking being, the doing being,
the feeling being.
We bless you, God, for your Triune Self:
the Triune who creates,
the Triune who takes flesh,
the Triune who empowers.
Thank you for your presence in sun and water,
in humanity and all Creation.

Morning Prayer

We arise today

in the goodness of Creation.

We arise today

in the verdure of the fertile ground.

We arise today

in the promise of the rising seed.

We arise today

in the joy of baby animals, the energy of rivers,

and the power of the thunderstorm.

We arise today

in the quiet strength of trees,

the abandon of falling leaves,

the transformation of butterflies,

and the eternal hope of the

Earth's changing seasons.

We arise today in you, the Living One.

Creator God

God of life, you summon the day to dawn
and call us to create with you.
You are the Rock from which all earth is fashioned.
You are the Food from which all souls are fed.
You are the Force from which all power lines travel.
You are the Source who is creation's head.
You are the Heart from which all hearts are beating.
You are the Mind from which
come thoughts and dreams.
You are the Eye from which comes all our seeing.
You are the Gift from whom all mercy streams.
You are the Ache from which comes all our longing.
You are the Pain in which we bear our grief.
You are the Wind by which all souls go winging.
You are the One from whom flows all our life.

The Humility of Earth

We arise today
in the simplicity of the empty soil,
in the strength of the fierce elements,
in the deep formation of winter.
Stripped of inessentials we stand, rooted in you.
In the anticipation of gathering strength,
you sustain our well-being.
In the humility of the bare earth,
we invite you to do your work in us.

Welcome God's Grace

Glad Bringer-of-Brightness,
day's blessing, rainbow's embrace,
teach our hearts to open as the buds open
and to welcome in your grace.
Teach us to dance with the playful clouds
and to laugh with sun's smile on our face.
The Earth is yours; may it bring forth its produce.
The birds are yours; may they
bring forth their songs.
Our work is yours; may it bring forth its yield.

Jesus the Seed

Jesus, you taught that we
can only fulfill our calling
if we become like a seed that dies,
buried in the earth,
in order that many new ones may grow.
Give us courage to be brave as seeds,
as humble and hopeful,
like you.

III
LOVE'S RESULTS

Full-grown love throws fear away.
—1 John 4:18

*Once a person learns to read the signs of love
and thus to believe it, love leads
them into the open field
wherein they themself can love. . . .
[They are] not the one who has to bring
themself into line with God;
God has always already seen in them a beloved child
and has . . . conferred dignity upon
them in the light of this love.*
—Hans Urs von Balthasar (twentieth century)

9
RENEWAL

When you send forth your breath,
you create us anew,
and you renew the Earth.

—Psalm 104:30

Paul consoles his hearers by saying
"renew yourselves" from day to day.
This is what we do with houses:
we keep constantly repairing them as they wear old.
You should do the same thing to yourself.
... Have you made your soul old?
Do not despair, do not despond
but renew your soul ... and never cease doing this.

—John Chrysostom (fourth century)

Spirit of Renewal

Spirit of God, among the wheels of industry,
renew the face of the Earth.
Spirit of God,
among the computers of commerce,
renew the face of the Earth.
Spirit of God,
among crime-infested neighbourhoods,
renew the face of the Earth.
Spirit of God, among tired and broken families,
renew the face of the Earth.
Spirit of God, among the lonely and the sick,
renew the face of the Earth.
Spirit of God, among the drugged
and disillusioned,
renew the face of the Earth.

Infused with the Spirit

Spirit of the living God,
anoint our creativity, ideas, and energy
so that even the smallest tasks
may bring you honour.
When we are confused,
guide us.
When we are weary,
energize us.
When we are burned out,
infuse us.
Renew us with your life.

The Power of the Spirit

Release in us the power of your Spirit
that our souls may be free to roam
your boundless stretches of space.
May we soar high like the eagle,
see horizons yet undreamed of,
glow with fires of compassion,
and flow with streams of creativity.
Breath of God, blow away all
that impedes your love.
Breeze of God, refresh our tired frames.
Wind of God, blow us where you will.
Dew of God, refresh our tired routines.
Rain of God, revive our withered lives.
River of God, flow through us and heal our land.

Make All Things New

Among the hungry,
among the homeless,
among the friendless,
come to make things new.
Among the powerful, among the spoilt,
among the crooked,
come to make things new.
In halls of fame, in corridors of power,
in forgotten places,
come to make things new.
With piercing eyes, with tender touch,
with cleansing love,
come to make things new.

More Like Christ

Christ,
you are the refined molten metal
of our human forge.
Purge our desires,
strengthen our resolve,
sharpen our minds,
shape our wills,
renew our energy.
Make us more like you,
the perfect expression of humanity.

The New Life of Christ

Let the cares of the past grow dim;
let the skies and our hearts grow clear,
as the Child of God comes striding towards us,
walking on this earth,
bringing new life.

The Waters of Renewal

O Christ,
you entered the stream of human life:
immerse us in the Divine life.
Immerse us in the waters that cleanse.
Immerse us in the waters that
overwhelm selfishness.
Immerse us in the waters of creativity.
Immerse us in the waters of renewal
and life everlasting.

Renewing Light

Shed light upon our brow
and on what we grow.
Shed light upon our cheek
and on what we seek.
Shed light upon the seeds
and on our deeds.
Shed the light that renews
like morning dews
our hearts and minds,
our flesh and souls.

Creator Spirit

Creator Spirit, come,
renew the face of the Earth.
Kindling Spirit, come,
inflame our waiting hearts.
Anointing Spirit, come,
pour into our lives afresh.

Renewal in Sleep

As we enter into sleep,
keep our souls, O Creator, keep.
As we enter into rest,
renew our frames, O Saviour blest.
When we wake with work to do,
Holy Spirit, see us through.
Holy Three, our shield, our wall,
be our rest, our joy, our all.

Alleluia!

You are the Food
from which all souls are fed;
you who gave birth to the universe
are born again in us;
you who brings renewal
after each disaster,
bring new life to our broken hearts.
Alleluia!

To the Very End

O God, when the ride is bumpy
and the world passes me by,
you pour out your life for me,
right to the very end.
When I am edged aside
and doors are shut in my face,
you pour out your life for me,
right to the very end.
When others are out to get me,
and my home is not secure,
you pour out your life for me,
right to the very end.
When my life is but a flicker
in the darkness that encroaches,
you pour out your life for me,
right to the very end.

All Things Made New

Risen Christ,
give us your resurrection eyes
to see eternity in a grain of sand
and God in a gang of troublemakers;
to see fresh flowerings in worn-out places
and fresh life in burned-out believers.
Risen Christ, come to make all things new.

10

WALKING IN THE PROMISE

All the promises of God are YES!
Through God comes AMEN, the inflection point of truth,
bringing to light the glory of God through us.

—2 Corinthians 1:20

When the presence of God emerges
from our inmost being into our faculties,
whether we walk down the street or drink a cup of soup,
divine life is pouring into the world.

—Thomas Keating (twentieth century)

Faith is not just a matter of hope and optimism. . . .
It's the courage to believe that God will
do what [God promised],
the courage to make peace with being misjudged
when others don't understand the path you're on,
and the courage to stick with it,
even when you don't understand the details yourself.

—Andrena Sawyer (twenty-first century)

Waiting for the Promise

With Abraham and Moses,
waiting to be led to a place of promise,
we wait.
With Amos and Hosea, Isaiah, Micah,
and all the prophets who believed
you are a God of justice,
we wait.
With Paul and Silas,
and all God's people imprisoned and persecuted
for acting on their faith,
we wait.
With Naaman and Jairus,
Bartimaeus and the Syro-Phoenician woman,
longing for an end to pain and rejection,
we wait.

With Zacchaeus in his tree
and the Samaritan widow at the well,
keen to be liberated from a half-life,
we wait.
With Sarah and Hannah, Elizabeth and Mary,
looking forward to new life and new beginnings,
we wait.
With Jesus in the desert and in the garden
because he asks us to,
we wait.

(echoes a prayer of the Wild Goose Resources Group)

Ruler of Promise

Ascended Lord,
you have made us living stones
of the temple you are to build.
We offer all that we are
and all that we have
to you.
Ruler of Glory: ennoble us.
Ruler of Grace: cherish us.
Ruler of Life: renew us
Ruler of Promise: surprise us.

Believers in Divine Promise

When we are lonely,
may we, like your servant Antony,
believe in your promise of human friendship.
When we are discouraged,
may we, like your servants Abraham and Sarah,
believe your promise,
even when it seems impossible.
When we, like your servant Hannah,
feel we don't measure up to society's expectations,
may we believe your promise
of new and unexpected birth.

(Antony, one of the Desert Fathers, lived alone in the remote areas of Egypt; God promised him connection with a kindred spirit, which was fulfilled when Antony met Blessed Paul, another hermit. God promised a child to Abraham and Sarah, and also to Hannah; in their old age, Abraham and Sarah gave birth to Isaac, and Hannah became the mother of Samuel.)

Participating in the Promise

We give you thanks for your ancient promise
that while the Earth endures,
seedtime and harvest, cold and heat,
summer and winter, day and night,
will never cease.
We thank you for light,
without which nothing would grow.
We thank you for water,
without which plants would wither.
We thank you for air,
without which all would die.
Light of light, Source of water,
Breath of life, You are here.
May we renew your promise to the Earth.

Promises Fulfilled

Come, O Spirit of Love,
that goes to any lengths,
that breaks through a lifetime's crippling habits,
that wells up from the depths.
Come, O Spirit of Joy,
that brings a song into haggard lives,
a serenity into our roots
and a sparkle into our eyes.
Come, O Spirit of Peace,
that heals mistrust
and brings us into harmony
with the still center of the universe.
Come, O Spirit of Kindness,
that delights to sweeten the lives of others
and do beautiful things for God.

Come, O Spirit of Goodness,
that opens the heart to Christ
in friend and stranger.
Come, O Spirit of Gentleness,
that bears all things without
harshness or hardness.
Come, O Spirit of Fire,
that burns away selfishness and
double-minded ways.
Come, O Spirit of Wisdom,
that teaches us to see into the nature of things
in order to know, speak and do what is right.
Come, O Spirit of Power
that snaps the chains of fear
and casts out the demons of hell and hopelessness.
Come, O Spirit of Faithfulness,
fulfill your promises in our life.

11
ETERNITY

The is the life that never ends:
knowing you, the Supreme One,
who sustains all things.

—John 17:3

If your whole soul has become a spiritual eye,
and your whole soul light;
and if you have been nourished with the Spirit,
and if you have drunk of the Living Water,
and if you have put on the garments of the ineffable light;
if your inner being is established in the experience
and full assurance of all these things,
behold, you live! You live the eternal life indeed,
and your soul from henceforth is at rest with God.

—Macarius of Egypt (fourth century)

Don't fear the death of that which is known.
If you die to the temporal, you will become timeless.

—Rumi (thirteenth century)

Eternal Life Even in the Darkness

Into our place of darkness,
into our place of strife,
into our fears and worries,
come with eternal life.
Into those who are dying,
into those weary of life,
into those lost and despairing,
come with eternal life.

Through All Eternity

You who clothes the flowers
and feeds the birds of the sky,
who leads the lambs to pasture
and the deer to water,
who multiplied loaves and fishes
and changed water into wine,
lead us, feed us, multiply us
and change us,
until we reflect
the glory of our Creator
through all eternity.

Prayer After a Death

God of eternity,

from you we come;

to you we go.

Have mercy on those who have gone.

Give peace to us who remain.

Eternity's Child

Child of the prophets, on our longings
    let your light shine.
Child of Mary, on our littleness
    let your light shine.
Child of Eternity, on our lying down
    let your light shine.

The Bridge

Jesus, you are the glory of eternity
shining among us,
the tenderness of God
here with us now.
Jesus, you are the Healing Person,
the pattern of goodness,
fulfilling among us the highest human hopes.
Jesus, you are the champion of the weak,
the counsellor of the despairing,
the brother of us all,
who knows our every need.
Jesus, you are the splendour of the Father,
the Son of Mary,
our Bridge between this life
and the world beyond.

Ingathering

Since it was you, O Christ,
who bought each soul—
at the time it gave up its life,
at the time of severing the breath,
at the time of returning to dust—
may your peace be on your ingathering of souls.
Jesus Christ, Son of gentle Mary,
your peace be upon your own ingathering.

(echoes Carmina Gadelica)

Eternal Fruit

May the Creator, the Saviour,
and the Sustaining Spirit
bless the Earth and all that grows on it;
bless your soul and all that comes from it;
that you may bring forth fruit
on earth and in eternity.
Amen.

The Divine Presence

Eternal Light, shine into our hearts.
Eternal Goodness, deliver us from evil.
Eternal Power, strengthen us.
Eternal Wisdom,
scatter the darkness of our ignorance.
Eternal Compassion, have mercy on us.
With our whole being we shall seek your face
until we are brought into your holy presence
for eternity.

Droplets of Eternity

We come to you, God of surprises,
alert and watchful.
Awaken in us awareness of our origins in you,
and the needs of the world,
that droplets of eternity may fall
from us on this Earth.
Make us sensitive to the motions of your Spirit—
in our souls, in the faces of others,
and in the meetings we did not expect.
May we recognize that we live surrounded
by eternity.

The Silence of Eternity

Word of God,
out of the silence of eternity
you ceaselessly speak to your children.
Teach us to listen,
not to the discordant babble of a sick society,
but to the treasures of truth
in the deeps of silence.

The Working of Eternity

The Holy Three encircle you.
The Saving Three release you.
The Eternal Three keep you.
May the Loving Three caress you
and work in you,
in your loved ones,
and in those you have lost;
in your dark, in your day,
in your pain, in your joy,
in your blindness and in your seeing,
in your journey,
in eternity.

The Keeper of Eternity

Now let us praise the Maker of Heaven,
the Crafter of the starry skies,
the Keeper of Eternity.
Now let us praise the Birther of Glory,
the Guardian of the human race,
Uncreated Beauty
who binds the universe in one free bond of love
forever.

More books on
Celtic spirituality from
RAY SIMPSON . . .

(All are available from AnamcharaBooks.com,
Amazon, and most online booksellers.)

The Celtic Book of Days

Ancient Wisdom for Each Day of the Year from the Celtic Followers of Christ

The ancient Celts found God's presence in each ordinary moment of the day. Everything they encountered revealed to them the presence of the sacred; each day was deep with meaning. Now you too can practice the Celts' faith, as you take a few moments to immerse yourself in their wisdom. These small daily moments of reflection and insight will open your heart to each day and all it holds.

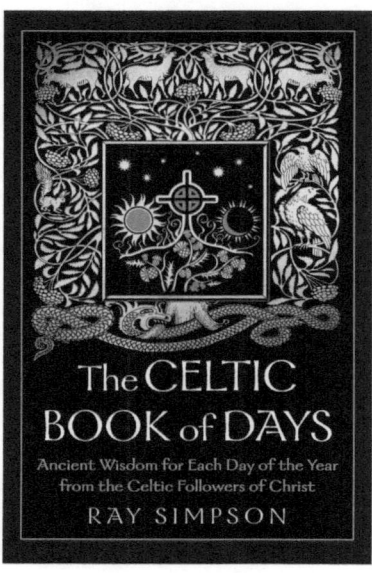

This day I call to me

God's strength to direct me,

God's power to sustain me,

God's wisdom to guide me. . . .

God's sheild to protect me.

(Saint Patrick)

Celtic Christianity
Deep Roots for a Modern Faith

The world of the long-ago Celts appeals to many of us in the twenty-first century. Whether we are looking to find our cultural heritage or are seeking an alternative to worn and restrictive religious forms, the earth-centered, woman-friendly, inclusive faith of the Christian Celts offers us a deep-rooted alternative approach to traditional Christianity. The Celts experienced "thin places," where they sensed the supernatural world; they honored their poets, singers, and artists; and they passionately followed the Christ of the Gospels. Theirs was a church without walls, which lived naturally and comfortably within the community. Ray Simpson has spent most of his life walking in the footsteps of the Christian Celts, and now he allows us to experience for ourselves their dynamic spirituality.

Soul Friendship in the Celtic Tradition
Ancient Insights for Today

The special friend who accompanies a person through life's journey is more precious than gold. The early Christian Celts had a heartwarming name for this person: the Anamchara. (Anam is the Gaelic word for soul; chara is the word for friend—"friend of the soul.") This special friend was someone with whom a person could talk through practical matters, reveal hidden intimacies, and break through the barriers of convention and egotism to an eternal unity of soul.

Ray Simpson brings this ancient concept into the twenty-first century, drawing practical applications from the long history of soul friendship. He describes a spiritual bond that lasts beyond this life into eternity, for it flows directly from God, who is the pattern of all friendship, the center and source of all human relationships.

Dance of Creation

Celtic Prayers of Celebration and Insight, Repentance and Restoration

In the prayers collected in this book, Ray Simpson asks us to "hear the cry of the earth and work together to 'choose life'" (Deuteronomy 30:19). He reminds us that Divine life courses through Earth's rivers, breathes through her winds, and sings in each life form she nourishes, and he invites us to celebrate Earth's beauty as we learn from her deep wisdom. At the same time, with a prophet's clear voice, he calls to us to repent of our selfishness and ignorance, and commit ourselves to the Earth's healing and restoration. "Come!" he says. "Celebrate! Learn! Repent! Take hands and work together! Join in Creation's dance with all your strength and soul!"

May every soul join with the song Nature sings. May the birds sing, may the trees clap, and may we humans taste and dance.

Celtic Prayers for the Rhythm of Each Day

We sometimes think prayer belongs only in certain places on certain days. This book calls us to set prayer free from these constraints, allowing it to flow out through the hours of every workday, sanctifying the ordinary rhythm of our modern lives: waking up, going to work, breaking for lunch, ending the workday, the evening hours, and going to bed.

Ray Simpson gives us twenty original prayers, written in the Celtic tradition or patterned after ancient Celtic prayers, for each of these intervals. Like generations of earlier followers of Christ, we too can use prayer to bless the rhythm of our daily lives, infusing the hours with the awareness of the One who gives us Life. These small pauses throughout the day will make us ever more aware that the Kingdom of Heaven is a constant and present reality, hidden just beneath the veil of everyday life.

Paths of Justice
Celtic Prayers for a World of Equity, Unity, and Healing

*Energize us with Your compassion, Giver of Life,
to help the dispossessed, to listen to those without voices,
and to reach out in friendship to all.
Empower us with Your love; encourage us with Your Spirit;
make us strong to bring Your justice
to individuals, communities, nations, and the entire globe.*

Our society often assumes that "justice" has to do with punishment. We think it means we make criminals pay for their crimes. The biblical meaning of the word "justice," however, means "to make right."

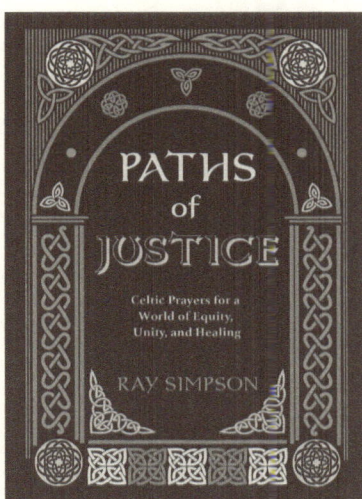

This concept of justice has to do with healthy relationships based on equity and kindness; it refers to a society based on life-giving relationships between God, human beings, and the natural world. This is the world Ray Simpson seeks to build, and he offers these prayers as openings into the Divine power that constantly seeks to heal and restore.

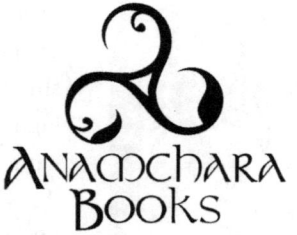

AnamcharaBooks.com

www.ingramcontent.com/pod-product-compliance
Lightning Source LLC
Chambersburg PA
CBHW060525080526
44586CB00012B/619